A FIRESIDE BOOK   PUBLISHED BY SIMON & SCHUSTER

SINGAPORE   TOKYO   SYDNEY   TORONTO   LONDON   NEW YORK

Brian Browne Walker

NEW YORK   LONDON   TORONTO   SYDNEY   TOKYO   SINGAPORE

A FIRESIDE BOOK   PUBLISHED BY SIMON & SCHUSTER

A FIRESIDE BOOK   PUBLISHED BY SIMON & SCHUSTER

NEW YORK   LONDON   TORONTO   SYDNEY   TOKYO   SINGAPORE

The **CRAZY Dog** Guide to **Happier Work**

NEW YORK   LONDON   TORONTO   SYDNEY   TOKYO   SINGAPORE

A FIRESIDE BOOK   PUBLISHED BY SIMON & SCHUSTER

FIRESIDE
Rockefeller Center
1230 Avenue of the Americas
New York, New York 10020

FIRESIDE and colophon are registered trademarks
of Simon & Schuster Inc.

Designed by Songhee Kim
Illustrations by Stuart Cameron Vance
Manufactured in the United States of America

1   3   5   7   9   10   8   6   4   2

Library of Congress Cataloging-in-Publication Data is available.
ISBN: 0-671-86573-0

Livication

~~~~~~~~~~~~~~~~~~~~

This book is livicated to the eternal
illuminating presence of Robert Nesta Marley —
tuff gong, rastamon, prophet of God.

"Jah lives, children."

We refused to be
    what you wanted us to be
we are what we are—
That's the way it's going to be,
    if you don't know.
You can't educate us
    for no equal opportunity.
Talkin' 'bout my *freedom*, people—
Freedom and liberty!

We've been trodding on the wine press
    much too long—
Rebel! Rebel!
We've got to rebel, y'all . . .

        —Bob Marley, "Babylon System"

◎   ◎   ◎   ◎

Acknowledgments

My first bow must be to my father and mother, Bud and Joan, who through their consistently loving and honorable examples taught me more about this subject—and everything else—than I can say.

Wendell Berry, Jim Harrison, Stephen Mitchell, and the family of Bob Marley allowed me to sample their exquisite songs here, for which I give thanks and praises. Handsome Stuart Vance survived a late-round knockout on an earlier project and rose from the canvas to illustrate this book, and I'm glad of it. My brothers Marc Macaulay, David Grimes, Evan Ward, Martin Gray, and Patrick Gorlick helped me become the dangerous lunatic I am today; thanks, fellows. Finally, thanks and praises in all 10,000 ways to Jah, Ma, Pa, Laurie Lysle, Julie Bird, Valerie, Cincie, Sasha, Sosie, Max, Grandfather Ed, Chief Peyote, and my kidguru Sofia Sofia Muhammad Ali, formative influences one and all.

◎   ◎   ◎   ◎   ◎   ◎   ◎   ◎   ◎   ◎

Greetings!

If you aren't as happy as you would like to be in your work — if you'd like to get a dazzling new job, or discover a way to make your old job fresh and vital and exciting again — then you've found your way to the right book.

Let's get right to a couple of important principles.

PRINCIPLE #1: Work Is Hell

Dogs don't do it, ducks don't do it, and dolphins don't do it, all for the same good reason: working ain't natural. And it's no more natural to humans than it is to any other creature. We were designed to wander around, picking berries, making love, and swimming under warm waterfalls, and that's exactly what we did for ninety-nine percent of our history. Then, in a blink of the evolutionary eye, along came agriculture and capitalism and science and technology — terrific, desirable things, were they not accompanied by time clocks, stiff shoes, fluorescent lighting, neckties, and income tax. Things went to hell in a handbasket in a genuine hurry: you can't dance, sing, or go swimming with your sweetheart if you're punching numbers into a computer in some gray little office. And that, in a nutshell, is why work is hell.

◎   ◎   ◎   ◎   ◎   ◎   ◎   ◎   ◎   ◎

PRINCIPLE #2: Work Is Heaven

Back to dogs, ducks, and dolphins: what's cool about them is that they live in a state of fluidity, dancing from one moment to the next, always attending to what's in front of them without a care about what has gone by or what is yet to come. Work, for all its potential pitfalls, offers that same opportunity: a chance to be so absorbed in something that you lose yourself completely, like a child at play. All boundaries dissolve, and you become the activity itself.

The best work *is* like the play of children: it gives us a chance to fall into a dance with others, to build things that are good, to make a happy mark upon the world. And that is why work can also be heaven.

PRINCIPLE #3: Heaven or Hell— It's Up to You

I have worked with a great many people in a wildly unusual assortment of jobs, but one thing was always the same: most people I knew were discouraged by their experience of work. They regarded the notion of finding happiness in their work as difficult and complicated, if not altogether impossible.

◎   ◎   ◎   ◎   ◎   ◎   ◎   ◎   ◎   ◎

The truth is that having happy work is relatively simple. One has to deal with only two things: the actual work one does, and the spirit in which one does it. If you tackle just these two things head on, then happier work will be yours.

About the Title of This Book

The title of this book comes from an old Crow Indian idea called Crazy Dog activities. The Crow believed that when one's life fell into a rut, one had to go a little bit crazy to make things fresh again. A Crow practicing the Crazy Dog way might start doing everything backward—sleeping during the day and eating break-fast for dinner and riding facing the tail of his horse—or he might go wacky on a grander scale, dragging a dead dog around on a rope for a week, or galloping, naked and blindfolded, downhill through thick trees.

You don't have to take a dead Dalmatian to the office to benefit from the Crazy Dog way in your work. The activities in this book are more subtle, but their objective is the same: to bring you fully into the moment. Being completely *here*, right *now*, has one of two effects: either you lose yourself in the flow of what you're doing and fall in love with it again, or you discover why you came there, so you can absorb the lesson and move on. This book will lead you to one place or the other.

About the Use of the Word "God"

You will see the word "God" in this book. I use it because it works for me in capturing the essence of a very high ideal, but I encourage you to substitute, if you wish, a word or phrase that works better for you. Other people use "my higher self," "love," "the greatest good," "the universe," or "the great and powerful Oz." In the end, I think they are one and the same; choose the one that suits you best.

My Promise to You

Here are thirty Crazy Dog activities. Do one a day for a month or so, and I promise that one of two things will happen. Either you'll find yourself more present, more alive, more aware—indeed, happier—in your current work, or you'll know for certain why you came to do that work, what you needed to learn from it, what kind of work you really ought to be doing, and how to be happy doing it. Sink yourself into this book for a month, and I promise you happier work will be yours.

Hoka hey!

Ponder the Horror

● ● ● If you want to shrink something,
you must first allow it to expand. ● ● ●

Tao te Ching

Imagine: A wheel comes off your car on the freeway and bounces past your window, rubber singing and hubcap winging away like a brilliant bird. Would you drive on, determined to have the car fix itself, or would you admit that something was awry and stop to investigate it? My guess is you'd probably stop, because everyone knows cars don't fix themselves. If you try to drive on when they're broken, it's just a matter of time until you crash and burn.

Well, work is the car that carries us through life, and it can crash if we don't stay on top of it by checking to see if anything's wrong and fixing it when it is. Today's Crazy Dog activity is to do the first part: to ponder, in short, the horror of your job. Quiet yourself and take a long, honest look at what you do for a living. What stinks about it? Where are the wheels flying off?

What are the things that you actually do during the day? Do you work in a public place, or talk on the phone? What are the people like whom you meet in your work? Are they unhappy to be dealing with you, or happy? Do you usually satisfy them, or do you more often frustrate them? Whom do you yell at? Who yells at you? Are your fellow workers carrying their share of the load? Truthfully, are you? If you don't deal with people, what *do* you deal with? If it's machinery, is it well designed and well maintained, or is it shabby? How does working with it make you feel about yourself? If it's food you work with, is it *good* food?

As you look at these things, be brutally honest with yourself. Look at them straight on, and don't pull any punches: what's at stake here is your one and only life. What do you hate about your job? How do you feel in the center of your stomach about the place where you work? Is it nicely designed and well lit? Is there fresh air? A nice view? How's the money? Are you fairly rewarded? Are you working too much or too little? How's the trip to work? How does the future look? Does it make you proud to tell people where you work and what you do, or would you rather not? Is there something you do that makes your stomach ache? How often do you have to do that?

Don't try to fix anything today. Just see what's wrong with clear eyes. You have a sense in your heart of where you would like to go with your life, and you know that you travel a lot of the time in a car called work. Today, point at the wheels that are flying off, making no judgments but carefully noticing each one. This is a step toward happier work.

◉   ◉   ◉   ◉   ◉   ◉   ◉   ◉   ◉   ◉

Wahoo! Poverty!

• • • The tides of meanness and poverty gather • • •
'round us, and, 'lo, creation widens to our view.

John Muir

As a child didn't you just love it when you were forced to do something you didn't want to do? Wasn't it a ball, being made to go to school every day and get dumb-looking haircuts and eat over-cooked brussels sprouts? You couldn't *wait* to grow up and escape being told what to do. Actually, if you're like most people, you're still being told what to do — only now it's your own thumb you're living under. It's the thumb that pokes you every morning and says, "Get up and go to that job no matter how you feel about it. You need *money!*"

Today's Crazy Dog activity is to kick the money habit: quit your job and embrace the pleasures of poverty. That's right — pick up the phone right now, call your boss, and say, "Listen, you swollen sack of fish farts, I quit!"

I'm kidding. Don't call your boss just yet. Instead, call yourself, and ask a few questions. Ask yourself if you do this job because

◎　　◎　　◎　　◎　　◎　　◎　　◎　　◎　　◎　　◎

you love it or because you need the money. Is this the kind of work you'd do no matter how well it paid, or are you only trading your precious time—your one and only life—for a sack of coins every week?

Ask yourself if this money is bringing you happiness, or if, in your heart of hearts, you even believe that money could do such a thing. Ask yourself how many rich people seem genuinely content. Most important, take a few minutes to think about the five happiest moments in your life: how many of them had anything at all to do with money?

The truth is, as any psychologist will tell you, that people become happy when they're doing what they want to do—not when they get a yellow Cadillac or a fur sink or a butler named Chowster. Yet most of us go on thinking that if the money dries up, we'll keel over and die, and so we go on doing things we don't care about.

Today, inside the quiet of your own mind, stop being a junkie to your job. Close your eyes and imagine leaving it behind for the last time and going home. *Really* imagine it. What happens to you? Do you die right off the bat? Or do you maybe—just maybe—suddenly feel a little more free? Can you sense a new lightness in your stomach, your heart, your body?

Look around at some of the things you've been spending so much money on. Which ones do you really need? Which ones satisfy something deep in you, and which are just distractions? Imagine letting the latter ones go—do you die right away, or feel a little more free? Does the world look a little different? Has creation widened to your view?

Sit inside this poverty you've created. Put it on like clothing, and see if there's anything about it that feels good—like, perhaps, the freedom to redirect your life in accordance with your deepest wishes, or the possibility of doing work of greater integrity.

Today, quit your job and embrace poverty. See how your vision of the world changes, and how it doesn't. Ask yourself: What is possible now? This is a step toward happier work.

The Reign of Mommy and Daddy

An important step in finding the way to right

livelihood is understanding why you do what you do right now, and

why you've done the things you've done in the past. An amazing number of otherwise self-realized people discover, when they look back at how they made vocational choices, that they were trying to please someone else: a parent, a beloved teacher, or perhaps their spouse. Today's Crazy Dog activity is to end the reign of Mommy and Daddy.

To achieve this, answer a simple question. (I suggest you write your answer down—writing has a wonderful way of clarifying one's thoughts—but it's not mandatory.) The question is this: Why do you do what you do?

Think back to how you chose the job or profession you're in. Who or what influenced you at the time? Did your parents always "plan" for you to become an engineer, or a nurse, or a business person? Did a career counselor push you into electronics because of "job opportunities" when what you really wanted to do was play music? Did you push your*self* into something unnatural in response to an unspoken pressure from your parents or a sense that you'd be making someone happy if you took this path?

Think back: How did you get to where you are? Perhaps you're not doing what Mommy and Daddy wanted you to do, but you made the grand compromise: you aren't doing what *you* wanted to do, either. How happy has it made you to devote your one and only life to carrying out someone else's plan?

Be straight with yourself about how you got to the job you're in. If what you discover is depressing, that's a good sign. If it isn't, you're probably letting yourself off the hook that this question is supposed to put you on. The Crazy Dog way demands courage from time to time, and now is one of those times. Ask yourself whose life you're living, and be rigorously honest when you answer.

Today, end the reign of Mommy and Daddy: determine how you got to where you are in your working life. This is a step toward happier work.

Who Feels It,
Knows It

Home is not a physical place but an emotional one. It is

where you feel completely calm and centered, where you give and

get exactly what you need, where you know in your very core

that you are where you should be. The way you sense you are there is with your heart. You *feel* it, and, as Bob Marley sang, "Who feels it, knows it."

Some years ago I used to work in the mergers and acquisitions department of an investment banking firm in New York City. I got up at five A.M., put on a suit and tie, worked long hours with tense people under impossible deadlines, and went home exhausted and depressed every night. I wasn't happy doing it, but I didn't know which way to turn. Late one night, though, a window opened, and I began to see the way home.

I had decided to shine all my shoes before I went to bed. Depleted and melancholy, alone in my apartment, I put on some music and sat in a comfortable chair and began the job, first lathering each shoe with saddle soap and then bringing it to a high shine with polish. After half an hour of quiet concentration, I stopped in shock and surprise: I felt genuinely and thoroughly *happy*, a feeling I had forgotten how to have.

I wanted to grab this feeling and hang on to it forever—you know how sexy happiness can be—so I immediately queried my heart: "What caused you to feel so good?" And my heart said to me, "Look around you, Brian. You're at home. It's quiet here, and you like that. There's music. You're wearing comfortable clothes. And look at your hands: You're working with them, doing something at your own pace to make a nice thing appear out of nowhere."

Who feels it, knows it. Today, I'm a writer: I work alone, in a place of my own choosing, wearing baggy old sweatpants and listening to weird music. My dog sits with her head in my lap, and when I want to stop doing what I'm doing—which is using my hands to try to make something nice appear out of nowhere—I just stop, scratch her behind the ears, and marvel at how good it feels to be home.

You have also had this feeling, or some part of it, and today's Crazy Dog activity is to remember what it was like. Close your eyes now, breathe deeply and slowly, and focus your concentration in your body. Ask it to remind you of the times when it felt most at home, the times when you worked with great calm and concentration, in a rhythm that comforted you, or in a place that made your spirit rise. They can be different times, or they can be times where one but not all of the pieces was present. The important thing is to get a sense of all the pieces.

Identify each of the components that has given you pleasure in work at some time. What were the sounds there? What was the light like? What kind of people—or animals, or trees—were around? What were you doing with your body? What did you wear? Say? Hear? Eat? Think? Feel?

For now, don't try to make anything of it. Just get yourself back to those moments and really remember what you felt there. Feel it in your body.

Who feels it, knows it. This is a step toward happier work.

Life with Honest Bob

How would you like to work all day with a used-car

salesman living inside you? Imagine it: A fat guy with a cheap wet

cigar and plaid pants named Honest Bob, who slaps you on the

back at crucial moments and hollers, "Come on! Don't worry about all those dadgum details! Let's make a *deal!*" And as you sign on the bottom line, he grins and winds back another odometer. How confident would you feel about your decisions?

Just about as confident as you feel now, perhaps because if you're like most of us you *do* have an Honest Bob in your life. He takes the form of that little voice that tells you it's okay to cut corners, to lie just a little or leave a detail out, to sell something crummy—in short, to do something that you know in your heart isn't right. Just because you can't smell the cigar doesn't mean he isn't in there.

In truth, Honest Bob is a fun guy. He helps you to play fast and loose, and he can be good at making a quick buck. But you'll never be truly happy in your work as long as you keep him around. Today's Crazy Dog activity is to begin the process of letting Honest Bob go.

Achieving this is very simple. All you have to do is ask this question about every single thing you do in your work: Is this honest? Start with the big stuff, like your job itself. Is it fundamentally honest? Do you provide a genuinely valuable product or service to people who truly want it? Did they want it on their own, or did you make them think they wanted it with a manipulative bit of advertising? Is the way you make your product or perform your service honest? Do you use materials that are honest? (Think of the earth as a living being when you answer that one.)

Is the price fair? Is the deal good for them *and* you, or is it good only for you? Are you becoming the man or woman you've always dreamed of becoming by doing this job?

After you look at your job, take a look at yourself. What about the *way* in which you do your job? Is it honest? Do you do what you agreed to do when you took the job? Is every movement you make during the day honest? Is everything you say honest? Are you honoring your ancestors, your God, your highest self in the way you do each and every thing you do at work?

If you can't answer yes to these questions and feel the truth of your answer resounding in your heart, then you have something that is dragging your work—and your one and only life—down. Let go of it now. Whether it's a job or the way you do your job, life will replace it with something better if you only let it go.

Today, flush the cigar, burn the plaid pants, and send Honest Bob packing. If it ain't honest, don't do it. This is a step toward happier work.

Him Goliath,
You David

~~~~~~~~~~

Don't you hate those impossible tasks? The

really big one, the boring, dreary one, the one that you put off

again and again, wishing someone else would do it, until it starts to

◎   ◎   ◎   ◎

look like a giant to you? Well, stop hating it, because it *is* a giant, and the giant's name is Goliath. You, in this once-in-a-Crazy-Dog-lifetime, today-only, offer-expires-at-midnight opportunity, get to be David.

You know this task when you see it, whether it's something you need to do in your current work or something you have to do to get the job you really want. The way you know it is that your mind turns and runs in the other direction at the first sight of it. "I'll do it tomorrow," you think, or "That's not really my responsibility," or "I think I hear my mom calling me." Today's Crazy Dog activity is to ignore those voices, pick up the slingshot, and take on Goliath. In other words, do the impossible: find the killer giant that no one (least of all you) wants to tangle with, and knock him to his knees.

Is there a filing cabinet that hasn't been organized since the Second World War? Take a deep breath, grin your best Crazy Dog grin, and dive in. Don't come out until the giant is dead, A to Z.

Somewhere, something is dirty, isn't it? So dirty that you and everyone else walk a wide circle around it for fear that the music will stop and you'll have to sit in the cleaner's chair. Today, knock the arm off the record *yourself:* roll up your sleeves, and clean like it's your passport to heaven. Don't forget the corners: it's clean corners that kill giants.

Maybe your Goliath is the need to tell the truth to someone about something. Steel yourself, breathe deeply, and talk straight. Remember: Only the whole truth slays the giant.

Is there a phone call that needs to be made? A relationship to be healed with an unhappy customer or supplier? Do you need fifteen percent more business to make it a great month? Today is the day: wind up that slingshot and let fly.

If you don't have a Goliath of your own, tackle someone else's. March up to the boss's desk and say, "What's the single thing you'd most like to have taken care of so you don't have to think about it anymore? I'm going to do it today." And then do it—every bit of it—absolutely as best you can, with all your concentration.

Slaying a Goliath is the best way to remind yourself that you have the power of a David. So take on a giant today, and when you've finished him off, write his name down. Look at it when you need to be reminded of your strength. This is a step toward happier work.

Become the Wood

I once watched a Native American man carving a

bowl from a piece of alder. It was a beautiful dance in which no en-

ergy was wasted. His movements were so smooth and centered, his expression so calm, his concentration so complete, that as the shavings piled up, it became hard for me to tell where the wood left off and the man began. He had, by focusing himself so absolutely into the activity, become the wood itself. Everything unnecessary was pared away, and what was left—of the man and the wood—was the essence.

Work that is done in a meditative fashion isn't work at all. It is a dance, a movement of pleasure and enthusiasm and balance, a renewing of one's self and one's relationship to the world. There is a simple way of bringing this dance into being: treat the work as yourself. See your job as a process that is shaping your spirit, a means of transforming the crude block of wood that you are into a graceful bowl. Today's Crazy Dog activity is to become the wood.

Whatever you do today, whether it is work that you think you hate, work that you think you love, or an effort just to get work, don't think of shaping the activity but of letting it shape you. See yourself as a piece of soft wood that is molded over the course of the day by the way you conduct yourself. Don't hack and chop; caress and stroke.

Do not rush what you do; neither should you drag it out unnecessarily. Breathe deeply, relax your body, feel for the proper

rhythm of the task. Concentrate carefully: how does the work want to be done?

Pay attention to each movement—how do you pick up the phone or the hammer, how do you use it, how do you put it away? How does this thing feel in your hand? Try to move like water. How does your body feel when you do this? If you *are* this work, this tool, this machine, how do you want to be handled? Knocked around, or made love to?

Is there some music in this task you can release by noticing it? How can you make this job, this person before you, this self of yours happier, right now, right here? What gentle thing can you say or do to release a tension? Notice that when you are gentle in your work, you are gentle in your self; sweet in your work, sweet in your self; calm in your work, calm in your self.

Today, as you do your shaping work, become the wood. This is a step toward happier work.

Settle the Mud in Your Glass

• • • There is no greater misfortune than having • • •
an enemy.

Tao te Ching

Let's face it, life is hard. Rent, politics, car payments, relationships, sex, drugs, and rock 'n' roll: we live in a complex world, a hurricane of fast-moving information, bewildering events, frightening changes. Somehow in the midst of it all we have to figure out, pretty much on our own, how to live well. There are times, no matter who you are, when life seems like a long dusty day stooping to pick thorns under a hot sun.

In work, however, as in love and laughter, we have a chance to drink a tall, cool glass of water along the way. Work can ground and center and give meaning and balance and satisfaction to life. It offers us, amid the inevitable trials of living, a chance to define ourselves, to do good, to share an effort of imagination and inspiration with our fellow human beings. It gives us a window into others and into ourselves that can teach us a great deal. At its best, work is a resting place under a willow tree, a moment in the shade with a glass of fresh water.

◎　◎　◎　◎　◎　◎　◎　◎　◎　◎

But it doesn't work that way when there's mud in the glass. Today, think of your work, and your attitude toward it, as a tall glass of water that you're going to drink. If there's mud in it, your Crazy Dog activity is to settle it.

Do you have an enemy at work? Someone whose presence makes your stomach tighten and tense? Someone you'd like to see get it good? It feels great to hate them, doesn't it? In the short term, nothing is more satisfying. In the long term, however, you've stirred a big glob of sticky mud into your glass.

Perhaps your enemy is yourself. Do you criticize yourself excessively at work, or cut corners, or avoid responsibility, or hate what you do? What gets your back up at work? The way your boss talks to you? Those uppity customers? That annoying thing you have to do every day at 3:15? There's mud in your glass.

You know how to find it without anyone's help. Just sit quietly for a moment and ask, "Is there mud in my glass?" When you see where it is, settle it. Heal the wounded relationship, forgive the unforgiven, release the long-held tension. Life is too long and too hot to drink muddy water. Settle the mud in your glass, and work with integrity and clarity and gentleness in every moment. This is a step toward happier work.

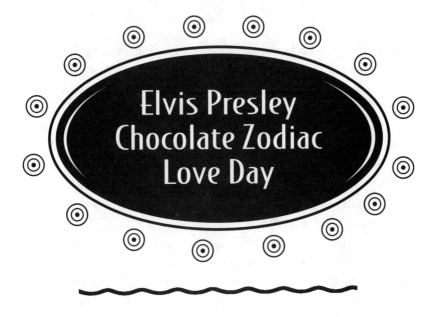

**Elvis Presley
Chocolate Zodiac
Love Day**

What if I said I had determined, through a complex

series of mathematical calculations, a generous amount of rabbit-

running and barking at the moon, and numerous consultations

◎   ◎   ◎   ◎

with celebrities both living and dead — including, but not limited to, Elvis Presley, Ernest Tubb, and Earl, the Fattest Man Who Ever Lived — that astrology is scientifically true beyond a shadow of a doubt? You'd believe me, wouldn't you? Of course you would.

And what if I said that Elvis appeared to me personally, driving a chocolate Cadillac, and read me your horoscope for today, and that it says, "Believe all the hype about yourself: today will be the best day of your working life." You'd believe *that,* too, wouldn't you? Of course not. But why don't you be a Crazy Dog for a moment and believe it? What would happen if it were true?

Would you ask for the raise you want and deserve? Would you get more work done than ever before? Would you make something especially fine? Would you laugh more than ever before with your fellow workers? Argue with them? Dance with them? Would you challenge the status quo? Would you ask — straight out, knowing that today anything you want is yours — for the job you've had your eye on? Would you simply *relax* into your work?

Go ahead and do it. Today's Crazy Dog activity is to pretend Elvis leaned out the window of his chocolate Cadillac this morning and whispered right in your ear, "Go for it, you good-lookin' thang."

This is the day to ask yourself, "Just what in the damn hell do I want anyway?" (If you never curse, be especially sure to do so now—it reinforces the Crazy Dog nature of what you're doing.) If you could have anything you want with respect to your work today, *what exactly would that be?* Answer that question, and then go out and get it. If your brain tells you it would like to help you but it just doesn't know how, thank it, and then ask your heart and stomach. They'll know; they *always* know.

What's been keeping you from really being your best? What project have you waited to start or finish or ask to work on or be in charge of? What were you going to ask for when the time was right? What were you going to bring to an end? A job, the way someone treats you at work, the way you treat someone else? Now is the time: it's Elvis Presley Chocolate Zodiac Love Day.

Pick only one thing, if you want, or pick a bunch of things. Just don't take on more than you can keep track of. And go after them one by one, so your focus is always concentrated on one achievement. Choose things that really count for you, because the stars are lined up to make this the best day of your working life.

Unleash yourself, because Elvis said to. This is a step toward happier work.

The Ten-Percent Habit

When you were a kid, did you ever have a

brother, sister, or friend who was a hog? Someone who had to have

it all, who wouldn't share, who thought his slice of pie was the big

round one? It made you feel cheated and abused, didn't it? And it probably made them feel guilty, in the long run, for having been so selfish.

Selfishness and greed don't work any better now than they did for us as kids; they are as damaging to a business or a community or a planet as they are to a family or a pack of friends. He who hogs the pie is doomed to a lonely life of stomachaches; he who shares, eats and lives in peace. Today's Crazy Dog activity is to begin the practice of cutting the pie and giving away a little before you eat your piece.

The practice of tithing is as old as civilization, and so is the magical number: ten percent. Throughout history and across many cultures, people have learned again and again the extraordinary benefits—to themselves, to others, to their society as a whole—of devoting ten percent of their income to helping others.

The greatest benefit of tithing accrues to the giver, and it is a psychological one. Immediately you'll see yourself in a new light: as a capable earner and a generous caretaker, a contributing participant in a family rather than one who only takes from it. An equally important effect of tithing is the meaning that it gives to one's work. Whether you dig ditches or design cars or act in movies, the

knowledge that your efforts are taking care of others as well as yourself—be they people, trees, or whales—transforms the work that you do. To give to others is, simply, to give to yourself.

There is another benefit to tithing: the more you give, the more you have. Everyone who practices it knows what I mean. Before you begin to tithe, you never have enough money; the bills pile up, you can't afford the things you want, you always feel squeezed. Once you begin the ten-percent habit—and it's important to train yourself to stick to it religiously—you find that you always have what you need, and you always feel clear and calm about money.

In the healthiest societies, tithing takes place on every tier: the individual gives, the business gives, the government gives. Then everyone is provided for and no one is wanting. If you can, get your company to adopt the practice and to involve all its employees in deciding where the money goes (in addition to the morale benefits, there's a tax benefit to giving ten percent of profits away). But most important, begin with yourself.

Write a check today, and celebrate the enlargement in your self. Be a Crazy Dog and embrace the ten-percent habit. This is a step toward happier work.

◎   ◎   ◎   ◎   ◎   ◎   ◎   ◎   ◎   ◎

Honor Your Buttocks

How long has it been since you made a big career

decision with your butt? Sounds ridiculous, doesn't it? But it

would've made perfect sense to the Crazy Dog Crow. They,

like most people who have lived close to the earth, had a different concept of intelligence than we do; they believed that intelligence resides as much in the hands and the heart as in the head. They knew that only by consulting one's entire range of senses could one accurately assess a situation and act with confidence.

If you think otherwise, try asking your brain to go to work one day while your butt sleeps in. It can't be done: the brain bone is connected to the butt bone. It's a system designed to work as a whole, and it works really well only when we acknowledge that and act accordingly. So today's Crazy Dog activity is to honor thy buttocks and work from your body, not your brain.

You might ask a few questions first. What do you do with your body in your work? Do you use its entire range of strength and movements, or do you park it in one position all day until it tightens and aches? Do you honor it by stopping periodically to stretch it and relax it and balance it? Do you direct your breath energy into its different parts? Do you feed it with love? Do you give it the sunlight and air that it wants?

What do your answers tell you about your work? Is this a job that's friendly to your one and only body? If not, is there a way to make it better? Maybe there's a job that would be better

for your butt, and maybe it would be better for you to find it.

As you work today, involve your entire body in what you're doing. If your job is to make decisions, try sitting quietly and consulting your body. Maybe the numbers on the page make your brain say yes—but what do your heart and stomach say? How do your feet feel about it?

If your job is physical, move your awareness all over your body as you work. What does your back say about the way you move? Too fast? Too jerky? How would your hips like for you to stand? Do your shoulders want to relax? Can you keep your breath deep and slow all day?

How do your ears feel around different people? What do you make of that? Is your butt happy? Be a Crazy Dog and ask it, "Hey, butt, what can I do to make you feel good?" Then do it, and see if your work satisfies you a little more.

As you work today, get into your whole body. Listen to what it tells you about your work, your attitude, your habits. Trust it—for a change—when it disagrees with your brain. The brain is clever, but the body is wise. Follow its advice when it tells you to rest or exercise or shake like a crazy muddy dog. Honor thy buttocks! This is a step toward happier work.

◎　◎　◎　◎　◎　◎　◎　◎　◎　◎

Let's
Get Lost

● ● ● Many of us apparently live in different worlds. ● ● ●
Do we see the same sky as Crazy Horse? Think of Anne Frank's
comprehension of the closet.

Jim Harrison

◎   ◎   ◎   ◎

The most dangerous idea you can have about your

work — or your life — is the idea that you know where you are.

The moment you begin to think that, your world shrinks tele-

scopically; mysterious and beautiful possibilities are eliminated

forever. The world is vast and unknowable, changing every minute,

always presenting us with new sights, sounds, sensations, and

combinations. How each of us views it determines whether the

sky is a living, breathing thing or a black hole, the closet, a tiny

prison or a comfortable home.

Our work is no different. As soon as we think we know what it
is — who we are as we do it, why we do it, what it accomplishes,
who the others are who are involved in it — it becomes a dead
thing. Only when we lose all these ideas can it really live and

◎   ◎   ◎   ◎   ◎   ◎   ◎   ◎   ◎   ◎

vibrate and hum for us. It is the encounter with newness and mystery and dramatic possibility that excites us in our jobs, and today's Crazy Dog activity is to jump off the path and get lost in the deep forest that is your work.

First of all, forget that you have a job, or that you're looking for one, if that's the case. Forget that you're paid for it, or that anyone expects you to do it, or that you have ambitions concerned with it. Pretend you're just meeting some friends to hang out and do some stuff together today.

Forget you know what that stuff is you do—and how you do it, what the result of it is, and whether you like doing it or not. Forget you know the people. Forget you know the plan. *Just get lost.* Spin around until you're dizzy, click your heels together three times, put a live chicken in your underwear, and take a look around.

You're lost in the woods: What does it smell like here? That person over there—is the important reason you came here not to do this work but to exchange some information or emotion with her? What is it? What about this task that you're doing now for the very first time—what's it like? How do you hold your body when you do it? How does it make you feel? Is there a faster way to do it? A sillier way? Pretend you fell asleep and woke up completely happy—what are you going to act like, right here, right now? Abandon that cramped little boat you've been living in and swim in the great, warm ocean.

Practice innocence. Forget that you're mad, bored, jaded, cynical, short-tempered, or in charge. Get off the path, shake yourself good, and take a look around. Be a child, and let your work become a fascinating garden. Is the sky alive? Whom do you love? Stop judging. Spin around, remember nothing, spin around again. Whom do you love now?

As Ryokan said

Abandon this fleeting world, abandon yourself,
Then the moon and the flowers will guide you along the Way.

Let's get lost today. This is a step toward happier work.

Blow
It
Out

When I was a teenager, I thought my car needed to be

"blown out" quite a bit. My buddies and I would drive around for a

while, looking for girls or trouble or whatever it is teenage boys are always driving around looking for, and then we'd all look at each other and say, "Whaddya think? Think it needs blowing out?" "Yep, I think we better blow it out." Then we'd drive out to a nice, long, straight country road and floor it: 40 . . . 60 . . . 80 . . . 100 . . . 120 . . . "There! All blown out—let's get back to business."

The idea, I guess, was that the engine needed regular vigorous exercise to stay healthy. I don't know that it really did, but it sure was a lot of fun. I *do* know that people need it: when we get clogged up in some way, when we don't shake ourselves good from time to time and get all the dust and leaves and cobwebs out, we can't work happily or well. So today's Crazy Dog activity is to blow it out.

Sit quietly and close your eyes for a moment. Look for something deep in you that needs to get out. It might be something having to do with work—a proposal you want to put forward, a relationship you want to clear up, a big push you want to make on a lingering task. But preferably it won't *be* your work, it will be something that's *keeping* you from working.

What's lurking there in the back of your mind, unspoken and unseen, every time you try to get some work done? Whom at home

or across the street or across an ocean do you need to talk to? Yell at? Cry with? Throw cold water on? Make love with? Throw cold water on *while* you're making love? Blow it out today.

What outrageous thing do you need to get out of your system? Should you go out to the airport and walk around singing in your pajamas for a while? Should you hike deep into the woods and yell at the top of your lungs until you can't anymore? Should you dance naked in your living room with the consenting adult of your choice? Is there a great practical joke you've been waiting to play on your best friend? Blow it out today.

Maybe something's stuck in the back of your mind. Is there a realization you need to have about yourself or your work or your family? Blow it out. What would you do for someone if you were going to do something *really* nice today? Blow it out.

Don't miss this chance to clean out your system. Figure out some place where it's sticking, then floor the accelerator, lean your head out the window, and whoop for all you're worth. Blow it out today so you can work free and clear, high above the clouds. This is a step toward happier work.

Remember:
You're Going
to Die

That's right. One fine day, you—yes, *you*—are

going to keel over and croak. Allow me to tell you more: soft

breezes will blow through the blossoms of spring, but you won't

◎   ◎   ◎   ◎

feel or hear them. Children will squeal with puppies in the park, but you won't be there to smile at them. Music will play, *sweet* music, but not for your ears. The stars will come out, and you'll not see them. Candlelit meals will be eaten, conversations will be had, and love will be made—but none of it by you. You will be in the ground, feeding worms and returning, like it or not, to dust.

Get the gruesome picture? Good. Think about it: Life is short, and there's nothing sillier than wasting it on work that doesn't matter. Today's Crazy Dog activity is simply to remember that you're going to die.

Make it real for yourself. Look at how much time has gone by in your life already. You hung out for a few days here and there, a few days turned into a few weeks, a few weeks turned into half your life. The other half—or third, or three-quarters, whatever's left—can evaporate in the same fashion. You don't pay attention to what you're doing, the days run together, and pretty soon you're sitting in a rocking chair with dribble running down your chin trying to recall whether you ate your Cream of Wheat or not.

If you think I'm being harsh about it, you're right. It *is* harsh. One day you'll fall over—BAM!—turn cold, and no longer be able to bite into fresh peaches.

◎   ◎   ◎   ◎   ◎   ◎   ◎   ◎   ◎   ◎

So think about it. This, as far as you can scientifically tell from here, is your one and only life. It took evolution a long time to make human beings, so you probably had to stand in a very long line—a few million years, anyway—to get to be one. What are you doing with it now that you're here?

Are you doing work that *counts*—to you, to others, to the world in general? Are you doing work that holds your interest, that makes you laugh and shake your head in wonder? Do you wake up eager, or are you intimately acquainted with the snooze button on your alarm clock? Press it a few more times, and your one and only life will be over.

If your work doesn't set you on fire, then today is the day to figure out what you can do to make it that way or to get work that properly inspires you. Only you can do this for yourself, and you'd better start now, because your last breath is around the corner somewhere, waiting for you, and you don't know how far away it is. And be cheerful about the fact that you figured this out now rather than after the fact.

Remember: You're going to die, so now is the time to lead a glorious life. This is a step toward happier work.

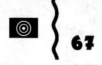

The human body, at peace with itself,
   is more precious than the rarest gem.
Cherish your body, it is yours this one time only.
The human form is won with difficulty,
   it is easy to lose.
All worldly things are brief, like lightning in the sky.
This life you must know as the tiny splash of a raindrop,
   a thing of beauty which disappears
   even as it comes into being.
Therefore, set your goal.
Make use of every day and night to achieve it.

                           —Tsong Khapa
                           Namche Bazaar, Tibet
                           May, 1979

Fresh Air

Doesn't it feel great when you come from a

hot, stuffy room into a breezy garden? Don't you love that

feeling of the fresh air hitting your nostrils, invigorating your body, and waking up your brain? There's nothing quite like it, is there?

Yes, there is—it's called "dissidence." Thomas Jefferson and Ben Franklin and Tom Paine were practicing it when they initiated the American Revolution. They challenged the status quo, and a great new nation came into being: fresh air. Abe Lincoln was being a dissident when he wrote the Emancipation Proclamation and abolished slavery. He turned something stale and rotten into something vital and alive: fresh air. Dissidence opened Eastern Europe, toppled the Berlin Wall, and ended the war in Vietnam: fresh air, fresh air, fresh air.

No organism can remain healthy without the fresh air of challenge and change. Not only countries but people and companies need challenges to question themselves, to redefine themselves, to grow bigger or better in some way. Today's Crazy Dog activity is to practice dissidence in your work and bring in some fresh air.

You don't have to march on the boss's office wearing a red bandanna and shouting slogans (although it would probably wake things up on the job, wouldn't it?). Begin instead by sitting in a quiet place, focusing on your work, and asking this question: "What could be different and better here?"

Is there a place in your work that makes you groan every time you get to it? A place where things stick? Something that's been done one way forever and should have been changed a long time ago? Today, be brave enough to point it out and argue for a better way.

Who's treating people badly? Who's ignoring an opportunity to make a change that will benefit everyone? Be an eagle today: swoop in close to them, beat your mighty wings, bring in some fresh air.

A little tip: in the words of the *Tao te Ching*, "Point but do not pierce." Take your example from the water that shapes rocks in the river. It knows where it wants to go and it confronts the rock directly, but it is also gentle, bending and accommodating the rock until it is worn away. Just don't be so gentle that you don't speak up at all.

Today, look around you in your work. Where is it dead, stale, musty? Ask "How can this be different and better?" Point to it, argue for it, blow fresh air on it. This is a step toward happier work.

Getting paid is great, isn't it? There you are,

toiling away, and somebody comes along and drops an envelope

full of happiness in your hand. You feel good about yourself and your work. Absolutely everything looks wonderful, doesn't it?—for a minute, anyway. That's the trouble with getting paid: it doesn't happen often enough or last long enough.

There's a good way around this, though. Get yourself a cheap revolver. Then, locate a convenience store late at night when no one is around. Next—no, don't do that. The food is bad in prison, and you never know who your dance partner will be. Instead, try today's Crazy Dog activity: get in the habit of looking all the time to see how you're getting paid.

Every moment in *every* job has a paycheck for you if you develop the knack of looking for it. Think about your own work today, and ask some questions about it. How many times during the day do you have a chance to learn something new? How many times can you have the satisfaction of fixing something that's not working? How often do you have an opportunity to laugh with a customer or a co-worker, or lay a reassuring hand on someone's shoulders? These are all paychecks, if only you'll stop to cash them. And the way you do that is by noticing them.

Think again about the happiest times in your life and how little they usually have had to do with money. The truth about happiness is that it *doesn't* have much to do with money—and that's as true in your work as it is anywhere else. If you're really going to love your work, it's going to come from something besides your salary.

The best place to get happiness is everywhere, since that's where it is. *Every* moment, *every* activity, *every* task and transaction, no matter how small or common, carries within it the greatest paycheck of all: an opportunity to feel joy.

For example, it feels *good* to help people, doesn't it? To send them on their way with their load lightened and a smile on their faces? Well, there are constant opportunities in every job to help others—and all you have to do is cash that check to take advantage of these opportunities.

Isn't it fun to kid people—or to compliment them, or to sass them a little? So kid, compliment, sass, cajole, humor, tickle, challenge, engage: cash every check.

Where else is there a check? Only everywhere. Can you remember to breathe into your heart during the trying moments of the day? There's a check; notice it and cash it. Can you make a graceful dance out of the way you move your hands as you cut off fish heads or staple forms or shift gears? There's your check; notice it and cash it. Can you remember that your work is your meditation and your prayer, a chance to see your highest self before you in the things you do and say and think? There is your check—and it's a big one—so notice it and cash it.

Today, look to see all the ways in which you're paid. Forget about money, and learn to cash *every* check. This is a step toward happier work.

Feedin'
da
Fellas

When I lived in Brooklyn, there used to be an auto

body shop nearby run by a fat, happy old Jamaican man named

Big Otis. Otis had a beautiful singing voice, and one day as I walked past on an errand, I was amused to see him standing on top of a car inside his shop, belting out a soulful rendition of "The Lion Sleeps Tonight." Everybody else in the shop was still working, but they were all grinning and grooving along. The man could *wail*, and you could see they loved it.

When I walked back by a half hour later on my way home, Big Otis was sweeping the sidewalk in front of his shop, and I asked him what had prompted the concert. "Ahh, you know, mon," he said, "I was jus' feedin' da fellas." Every day he sang like that to his crew, and it strikes me now that Otis knew a great deal about people and what makes them work well together. He knew that happy people do better work, and so he consciously poured some good energy into his employees every day. Today's Crazy Dog activity is to make like Big Otis and feed da fellas.

Take a boom box into work with you. Play "Little Red Corvette" real loud and climb up on your desk. When you've got everyone's attention, start yodeling and dancing and pulling your clothes off. When you're butt naked, jump down off the desk and start hugging everyone, saying, "I love you, man, I really do." Then work in the nude, smoking a big cigar, for the rest of the day.

◎   ◎   ◎   ◎   ◎   ◎   ◎   ◎   ◎   ◎

Okay, so maybe one or two of you will be unwilling to do that. Nonetheless, ask yourself this question: "What *can* I do to give the people I work with a good feeling today?"

Perhaps you'd prefer something subtle. If there's a company bulletin board, you could make a point of putting something on it every day. A good cartoon can change the direction of someone's bad morning; a "Quote of the Day" can be great for getting people talking or laughing.

Maybe you can follow a recipe to feed da fellas. Fresh-baked bread can make that cruddy office coffee taste wonderful, and when you hear someone groan, "Mmmmmm, that's *good*," smile and take pleasure. You've made a better place for you and everyone else to work, just like Big Otis did. And don't worry about whether anyone else is doing anything nice. Just be sure *you* do. Sooner or later, all good vibes are contagious.

Perhaps you could institute a picnic lunch in the park every Friday. Maybe you could bring flowers from your garden at home. Maybe you could pour warm spaghetti down your underwear during an important meeting—*I* don't know, *you* make it up. You know whom you work with, what they'll like, what's appropriate. The point is just to be conscious of giving them a little something every single day: a little cookie, a little music, a little love.

Today, be like Otis and feed da fellas. Make the place you work more of a home for everyone. This is a step toward happier work.

◎   ◎   ◎   ◎   ◎   ◎   ◎   ◎   ◎   ◎

Close the
Shame Drain

I didn't make this phrase up. I wish I could remem-

ber from whom I heard it, though, because it's one of the most

powerful ideas I know: Whatever you're doing that you're

ashamed of is a drain down which your vitality is pouring. Do it long enough, and your whole life goes down with a gurgle.

Shame is one of the most debilitating of emotions, and for good reason: it arises only when *we ourselves know* that we're doing something wrong. It is possible to get things done when you're carrying shame around, but it's not possible to really enjoy yourself. Even if everyone else thinks you're doing great, *you* still know in your heart of hearts that   thing's rotten, and, as the saying goes, "A house built on a weak foundation cannot stand." Today's Crazy Dog activity is to close the shame drain where your work is concerned.

What do you do in your work—or fail to do—that you are ashamed of? Does part of your job, or even the whole deal, require you to do something that doesn't feel right, that you wouldn't admire someone else for doing, that you wouldn't want your children or parents or your God to see you doing? If so, then the shame drain is open.

What about the *way* you do your work? Maybe the work itself is good, but there's a place where you're cutting corners—letting someone else carry your part of the load, or sweeping something under the rug, or simply not working with an attitude you feel

completely proud of. It shouldn't be too complicated to figure out. If you think about it a little, and you start to feel a gnawing inside—like you'd rather no one be watching or know this about you—then the shame drain is open.

Consider your reasons for doing the work you do, or want to do. Are you in it just for the money, or just to feed your ego, or because someone told you to do it and you didn't have the gumption to refuse? If so, the shame drain is open.

Today, ask yourself about every aspect of your work, "What am I ashamed of?" When you find it, fix it: close the shame drain. This is a step toward happier work.

The Whispers
of God Are
Heard as Daydreams

Many people stumble about in life,

moping that they would love to be happy in their work, if only

they could find out what they're *really* supposed to be doing. I

did it, too—I earned a Ph.D. in it during my twenties—but now I know this about it: it's bunk. You can easily discover—*today*—exactly what you ought to be doing in the world. And the way to do it is to pay attention to your daydreams.

All of us have two kinds of daydreams. The first are the Superman and Wonderwoman daydreams, the ones where you have billions of dollars and all the people who ever snubbed you are now begging to sleep with you, or at least go for a ride in your stretch limousine. These are entertaining, but they come from a part of your brain that is permanently sixteen, so let's ignore them for now.

The second class of daydreams is more grounded, more real. You can actually imagine yourself doing this thing, and, if you think about it a little bit, you can envision most or all of the steps you'd have to take to get there. It's okay if you think it's unlikely to happen, that you can't *really* have what you want. That's what you've been taught to think: "Don't run by the pool," "Go to school," "Be home by ten-thirty"—our culture *drums into you* the idea that you can't do what you want.

But in fact you can. You're a grown-up now, and you can run by the pool, quit school, and stay up as late as you want. You can also

live out your dreams—the second kind, anyway—if you learn to listen to them. And that's today's Crazy Dog activity.

What *do* you daydream about? Is there a certain level of success you fancy yourself having in your current work? Is there a completely different job or kind of work you'd really like to do? A certain feeling you imagine getting from your work? One that comes from working in a certain setting or with a particular kind of people? Now: Can you see most or all of the steps it would take to get there, even if it seems scary or impossible to think about taking them?

If so, then take a Crazy Dog leap: understand that this daydream was whispered into your ear by God Herself. *What you want to do is exactly what you are supposed to do.* And if you can imagine it, then it's possible to make it happen.

Today, listen to the whispers of God. Pay attention to your daydreams, and outline the steps between here and there. Start taking them, one by one, and keep taking them until you're standing in the middle of your dream. This—and this, and this—is a step toward happier work.

Weaken Your
Ambition, Strengthen
Your Resolve

The eighties were a great decade for ambition

in America. The pursuit of more money, more power, and more

stuff was elevated to the status of religion. The likes of Donald

Trump and Ivan Boesky were worshiped as near-deities—and that, to me, says something about the nature of ambition. When ambition is in vogue, the best people we can find to idolize are insecure braggarts, snide and contemptuous donkeys who waddle around braying about their fur underwear and sticking their names in big gold letters on everything in sight while their communities decay around them into a squalid soup of poverty, drug abuse, violence, and hopelessness.

Ambition is about "I, me, mine." Ambition says, "*My* ego is paramount. *My* fantasies must be fulfilled, no matter how bizarre. Damn everyone else; full speed ahead with *me, my, mine!*" Ambition can be a runaway train of greed and self-glorification, and today's Crazy Dog activity is to drop it like a bad habit.

Strong words, I know. After all, isn't ambition one of the cornerstones of the American way of life? Don't we need a ton of it to be successful in our work? I say it isn't, and I say we don't. What we want more of is not ambition, but resolve.

Let us look to an earlier decade and a greater hero: the sixties and Dr. Martin Luther King, Jr. For all their craziness, the sixties were good years for America, a time when we called into question some long-standing—and thoroughly rotten—things about our

country and ourselves. We acknowledged injustices in our society and in the world at large, and moved to correct them. We were led in this by people like Martin Luther King, who lived and worked from their hearts; who fought for the common good instead of common *goods;* who measured themselves not by the size of their bank accounts but by the weight of their contribution to family, community, nation, and world.

Today, take a look at the way you're working. Are you emulating Donald Trump, or Dr. King? Do you work from your head, planning and plotting and doing and getting, all to fulfill some notion you have about being important and powerful? Or do you work from your heart, going where you see a genuine need, doing what ought to be done, serving an idea that is larger than simple self-concern? Is your prayer "Let me get ahead," or "Show me how to do the right thing?" Are you sticking your name up in gold letters, or are you building genuine bridges in the world?

Today, work like your grandchildren are watching for clues on how to live in the world. Weaken your ambition, and strengthen your resolve. This is a step toward happier work.

◎   ◎   ◎   ◎   ◎   ◎   ◎   ◎   ◎   ◎

To: You
From: Your Friend Failure

My
Friend
Failure

There is no more pernicious idea in our culture

than the extremely popular notion that failure is bad. We live in

constant fear of failing in our work, failing in our relationships,

failing in our lives. And when we do fail, we act as though it were the end of the world. The failure of a deal causes one man to drink himself stupid; another yells at his family when he's fired from his job. We are taught, often through our competitive games and sports, that success is the *only* acceptable outcome and that failure is a fate worse than death. We imagine that in the best of all possible worlds everyone would succeed at everything all of the time.

I say different. I say that a life without failure is a life out of balance, a state where success has little impact because there is nothing to which it can be compared. I say that failure is a desirable thing, an important ally in work and in life, one of the wisest of our teachers. Today's Crazy Dog activity is to make friends with failure and accept the gifts that it gives.

Look at the places where you've failed in your work: the job that you didn't get, the job you couldn't do, the job that you lost. Ask yourself a few simple questions about your failure. What did you learn from it? What useful knowledge do you now carry with you wherever you go as a result of it? How many catastrophes have you avoided since you learned the lesson it taught you? How is your life actually better for all time for your having gone through this?

You may find it difficult to face these questions directly and answer them honestly at first. That doesn't mean the answers aren't there. It just means that you, like everyone else, have been so conditioned to fearing and avoiding failure that you've forgotten that most valuable of talents: learning from failure. So ask again, and again; look harder; listen more carefully: What gifts have your failures given you?

When I was younger, I nearly extracted a great fortune from the stock market, but I failed in a very big way at a crucial point. After a brilliant year, I greedily borrowed everything I could to try to get richer faster, and the market died a fast death, dragging my fortune into the grave along with it. I ended up owing money to everyone, including—yikes!—my girlfriend's father and one of my best friends. At first I wanted to crawl into the grave next to the stock market and my ex-fortune and have the dirt thrown over me. But I fought instead to make friends with my failure and to discover the gift that it came to give.

What I found when I looked was that my life had come to be about money, and that that was not a wholesome way to live. I saw that no one I knew who was obsessed with money was happy, and that I had been on a fast track to the same fate. Failure—painful,

gruesome, expensive failure—taught me to redirect my life, and every day now I'm grateful I lost all that money, because what I got back was my happiness.

Today, look back at your past failures, look now at your present failures, and look forward to future failures. Respect them, listen to them, and acknowledge the gifts they bring you in your life and work. This is a step toward happier work.

Confuse Yourself

Isn't it a wonderful treat to be bored? No,

of course it's not: our brains love new things, new challenges, and

new opportunities. The minute they've figured something out and done it long enough to prove it, they're ready to go on to the next challenge. Our hearts love new things too—the rush of fear at the appearance of the unfamiliar, the flowering of enthusiasm about meeting it, the resolve to understand it. And they, too, go back to sleep when a thing becomes old and familiar. Something about the design of human beings leads us to search out the fresh in order to keep our most powerful juices flowing.

For most of our history we satisfied that urge by living as nomads. We never knew what new delicious fruit or terrible animal lay beyond the next hill, and the suspense kept us going. These days, we have paltry substitutes like 150-channel cable television, which doesn't *feel* like living and never will. Where work is concerned, most people have entirely given up the idea of feeling alive and vital and charged from moment to moment. We *know* what's in store for us at work, and we sleepily trade our time for our paychecks. Our lives rush out; the money trickles in; and we expect little real stimulation out of the process.

It doesn't have to be this way. And today's Crazy Dog activity is to confuse yourself until your job begins smelling fresh again.

Start by looking at the Hopi. As one of the first Native American groups to stop wandering and begin practicing sedentary agriculture, the Hopi had to deal with the lack of the new. They came up with what is known as the left-hand meditations. The idea is simple: to make familiar things feel electric again by doing them in an unfamiliar way.

An elementary practice, the one for which these activities are named, is to use your left hand to do the things your right hand normally does, and vice versa. It doesn't sound like much, but try it. You'll see that your sense of time changes and your awareness becomes very focused on the task at hand. In the same vein, try doing something backward or upside down or at twice—or half!— the speed at which you ordinarily do it. Presto! Your brain is awake and you can feel your heart beat again.

How else can you confuse yourself? Close the office door, put on strange music, and think about nothing or daydream all day. Get up in the middle of the night and sit in the bathtub by the light of a candle to do the work you didn't do during the day. Make a funny noise every time you use your stapler or pipe wrench or printer. Wear your pants backward, walk funny, and use a bad fake accent when you talk on the phone.

Make it up yourself if you like, but go out of your way today to confuse yourself. This is a step toward happier work.

Forget the Forest and the Trees—Look at the Pine Needles!

Have you noticed how weary you get of looking at the same things over and over? That stupid blue car you bought, that goofball you thought was so good-looking when you got married, that dopey picture over the fireplace—they all get old, don't they? And when they do, one of two things happens: you get depressed and you wallow in it, or you get depressed and you do something extreme, like divorcing your spouse or buying a new car you can't really afford.

Work is like that. A job that seems like an enchanted forest at first soon becomes oppressively dull and routine. One day you wake up sick of filling out Form 32B, or the look on your boss's face, or the color of your office carpet. Your eyes glaze over, and you either quit on the spot, start smoking, or take amazingly frequent sick days. What you don't usually do is what you're going to do today, if you're Crazy Dog enough for it: forget the forest and look at the pine needles.

The pine needles are the little things around you, the "unimportant" ones that your brain automatically filters out: what the feet of your desk look like, how many numbers are on the *bottom* of the phone, whose shoestrings need replacing. Normally you're grateful to your brain for not bothering you with all this; today, ask it to bombard you with it, to throw off all the filters and show you what's around you, to make the forest enchanted again.

Ignore the boss's ugly brown suit—you've seen it a thousand times. Instead, notice the pattern of the stitching in the lapels, the number of buttons on the left sleeve, the angle of the pockets. Is there a tiny mustard stain on there anywhere? Look for pine needles.

What about turquoise? Is there any in the room? Is anyone whistling? How often does the coffee machine make that gasping noise? Watch the tip of your pen while you write—that's an intricate little dance that it does, isn't it?

How many light bulbs are in the room? How many are out? Who's got on mismatched socks? How many people in the room are left-handed? Can you hear music? What does the bottom right drawer of your desk smell like? How many erasers can you count from where you are? Who wears hair spray? Who has spinach in his teeth or a hair sticking out of his ear or toilet paper stuck to the bottom of his shoe? Is there a crack in the window? What spider weaves his web nearby?

Today, peel the glaze from your eyes and allow things to speak to you again. Look for pine cones and woodpeckers and leprechauns in the enchanted forest that is your job. This is a step toward happier work.

Dance
in
That Space

We hammer wood for a house, but it is the • • • inner space that makes it livable.

Tao te Ching

A job, like a house, has structural elements.

As a house has a floor, a job has certain hours for working:

structure. A house has walls and windows, a job has a boss and

co-workers: structure. A house has sinks and doorknobs and light

switches; a job has things like a salary, defined holidays, and

rules for how things are done and by whom: structure. A job

is also similar to a house in that while its structure defines the

appearance of it, it is the space inside it in which one actually

moves and lives and works.

The space inside your job is like the space inside your living room: it's the area available for you to move in within the structure that surrounds it. And just as you are free to decide what to do in your living room, you also have a choice about how to be in the space provided by your job. Today's Crazy Dog activity is to dance in that space.

Today, forget about how you look and what time it is and who is competing for what—forget the structure—and concentrate on how you are in your heart and body and mind as you work. Never mind *what* you're doing or *whom* you're doing it for or with or *how much* you're being paid to do it. Never mind the sound of the phone or the smell of the coffee or your ever-present judgments about what's going "right" or "wrong." Instead, pay attention to the empty space beyond all that, that place where you can move and think and feel any way you wish—and dance in that space with all your heart and soul.

Give up your cares for today about where this job is going, about who likes you and who doesn't, about your family and plans, your future and your past. Concentrate on your body in that space: move it as gracefully as you can. Concentrate on your heart: twirl it around, sing into it, breathe and laugh and let it expand until it's as big as the sky.

Today, don't sit in a corner all day grumbling and hitting yourself on the thumb with a hammer. Get up on your toes, mess up your hair, *dance in that space.* This is a step toward happier work.

Lick Your Finger and Check Out the Haps

Did you ever hear the street expression "What's the

haps?" It means "What's happening?" or "What's going on?" It's

usually used superficially, as a greeting and nothing more, but today's Crazy Dog activity is to deepen it — to ask yourself, "What's the haps?" and then pay very close attention to the answer.

My intention here is to remind you of one of your most fundamental powers: your ability to review the status of your life and calmly determine what needs to be done, if anything. Just as you lick your finger and stick it up into the breeze to determine its direction, or stick your toe into water to gauge its temperature, so also can you look at your life, check out the haps, and take guidance from what you see and hear.

With respect to your work, what *are* the haps? What's going on in your work life? Are you taking care of business and getting things accomplished, or not? Are you at war with anyone? In love with anyone? Taking advantage of anyone, or being taken advantage of? By what standard?

How does your brain feel about what you're doing? Is it excited, or sound asleep? What about your stomach? Is it quiet and relaxed, or all knotted up? How often do you use it for a belly laugh? How often do you pour medicine or alcohol or sugar into it?

How do your neck and shoulders feel? Loose and relaxed, or all welded together? Why do you think that is?

I suggest that you sit somewhere quiet for a few minutes and

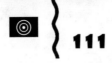

take a look at your work. What are the haps, and what do they say to you? Is there anything you need to do or say or change? Listen carefully to the voice that arises within you as you contemplate these things. Whether you actually hear it as a "voice" or not doesn't matter; each of us has a powerful self-guiding force at his or her center. If you'll only make a little quiet space for it, it will show you what's right and wrong, what things mean, what you need to do if something needs to be done.

Today, review everything that's going on in and around your work and how you feel about it. Then sit quietly for a while, listening. What's the message from inside? Wet your finger, stick it up into the wind, and check out the haps. This is a step toward happier work.

◎ ◎ ◎ ◎ ◎ ◎ ◎ ◎ ◎ ◎

Practice
Resurrection

Manifesto: The Mad Farmer Liberation Front
by Wendell Berry

Love the quick profit, the annual raise,
vacation with pay. Want more

◎   ◎   ◎   ◎

113

of everything ready-made. Be afraid
to know your neighbors and to die.
And you will have a window in your head.
Not even your future will be a mystery
anymore. Your mind will be punched in a card
and shut away in a little drawer.
When they want you to buy something
they will call you. When they want you
to die for profit they will let you know.
So, friends, every day do something
that won't compute. Love the Lord.
Love the world. Work for nothing.
Take all that you have and be poor.
Love someone who does not deserve it.
Denounce the government and embrace
the flag. Hope to live in that free
republic for which it stands.
Give your approval to all you cannot
understand. Praise ignorance, for what man
has not encountered he has not destroyed.
Ask the questions that have no answers.

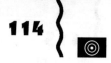

Invest in the millennium. Plant sequoias.
Say that your main crop is the forest
that you did not plant,
that you will not live to harvest.
Say that the leaves are harvested
when they have rotted into the mold.
Call that profit. Prophesy such returns.
Put your faith in the two inches of humus
that will build under the trees
every thousand years.
Listen to carrion—put your ear
close, and hear the faint chattering
of the songs that are to come.
Expect the end of the world. Laugh.
Laughter is immeasurable. Be joyful
though you have considered all the facts.
So long as women do not go cheap
for power, please women more than men.
Ask yourself: Will this satisfy
a woman satisfied to bear a child?
Will this disturb the sleep

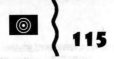

of a woman near to giving birth?
Go with your love to the fields.
Lie easy in the shade. Rest your head
in her lap. Swear allegiance
to what is nighest your thoughts.
As soon as the generals and the politicos
can predict the motions of your mind,
lose it. Leave it as a sign
to mark the false trail, the way
you didn't go. Be like the fox
who makes more tracks than necessary,
some in the wrong direction.
Practice resurrection.

Tomorrow, You're Canned!

What would you do if you woke up suddenly

and an ax were falling toward your forehead? Go back to sleep,

or do something about it?

Imagine that, in the boss's office, the decision has just been made to fire you tomorrow. It took them a while to come to it, but in the end it was clear: you're just not carrying your weight, not distinguishing yourself, not contributing anything of size or brilliance or importance. Regretfully, it's time to can you.

Now, figure out what you could do today to keep it from happening, and then do it. What might you do that would so impress them that they won't have any choice but to change their minds? What part of your work that you've been ignoring forever can you master today? What impossible task can you grab by the lapels and thrash? Grab it, then, and don't come up for air until it's done.

What's buried under dust? Liberate it, clean it off, oil it up, make it *sing* again. Show them the very *best* of what you're made of today, and show them so clearly that they pull you up off the chopping block and slap you on the back. But don't do it for the slap on the back. Do it for yourself. Use that imaginary falling ax as an opportunity to show yourself what amazing things you can do when you really have to, need to, or want to. Take a deep breath, work like a god, and don't stop until you're certain that you've

119

distinguished yourself mightily. The point, in the end, is to impress *yourself*.

Work today like the ax could fall tomorrow. This is a step toward happier work.

Simplicity
Is
Genius

The little black dress. The lever. The wheel.

What do they have in common? They're all perfect: perfectly

simple, perfectly effective. They are exceptions in our modern

culture, which is notable for its perverse attraction to difficult explanations and complex solutions. We couldn't be satisfied with simply gazing at the moon on a summer night when we had the option of building a billion-dollar rocket ship and taking a car up there to drive around on it. If something doesn't have bells and whistles and gizmos on its gadgets, we don't want it. If we can understand it, we're bored by it. If we can solve a political problem with a quiet conversation, we'd rather not—we're inclined to build a Pentagon and then go broke selling ourselves bullets at $12,000 apiece. Today's Crazy Dog activity, however, is to close the Pentagon and cultivate the genius of simplicity.

What in your work life cries out for a solution? A relationship, a machine, a shipping problem? Something that needs moving or cleaning or fixing? Today, return to the little black dress, the lever, the wheel: choose the simple solution.

What more powerful means of healing a relationship than a simple apology, a few kind words, a conciliatory smile? What better way of getting the responsibility you want than asking for it? What shorter distance between two points than a straight line?

Today, look at what you're doing, and if there's a simple way of making it better, *do it*. This is a step toward happier work.

Put Glasses
on Your
Blind Spot

Have you ever driven a car with a blind spot that

had you holding your breath when you changed lanes? Do you

know that feeling of tentativeness, that fear that your move into unseen territory will result in a loud scraping noise and public embarrassment? Do you ever have that same feeling in your work, a sense that there's a big part of the playing field that you're not even seeing, an anxiety that disaster is looming around a hidden corner? Today's Crazy Dog activity is to get rid of it by putting glasses on your blind spot.

The first step is to identify the area where you have this feeling. Is it in a relationship—with your boss, your assistant, or maybe everyone you work with? Is something out of kilter there somewhere? Or is it related to a specific part of your job? Perhaps you feel like you've never quite known what you're doing in this area. On the other hand, maybe the feeling is more general—an apprehensiveness about where your work in general is leading you.

Whatever it is, put your finger on it. Then, when you're sure you know where the fear-of-doom-blind-spot-blues are coming from, ask yourself a simple question: "What am I totally missing here?" Then sit quietly with the question until the answers come.

If your blind spot is in a relationship, look closely: What are you missing? Maybe it's something big—you're habitually treating people badly, and the negative energy is pooling up around you, giving you that feeling of a disaster in the making. Or is it some-

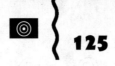

thing subtle, a small slight on your part that you can make right with a quiet apology or an offer of lunch in the park?

If it's some part of your work that's troubling you from behind a veil, what is it? Is there a better way to do something? A safer way? A quieter way, or a happier one? Do you really need someone else to do it along with you? Have you simply never learned how to do it properly in the first place? Is it the very nature of the activity that unnerves you? Be clear; put glasses on your blind spot.

Where *is* this work of yours leading? Take a few minutes to be quiet, and trust your vision to see down the road ahead—is that where you want to go? Do you need to change your course so that you end up in a place that you prefer?

Today, take the time to put glasses on your blind spot. Ask yourself, "What am I completely missing here?" and pay close attention to the answers. This is a step toward happier work.

Play Ball!

Let's look again at the words which opened this book:

> We refused to be
>   what you wanted us to be
> we are what we are—

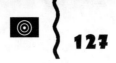

> That's the way it's going to be,
>   if you don't know.
> You can't educate us
>   for no equal opportunity
> Talkin' 'bout my freedom, people—
> Freedom and liberty!
> We've been trodding on the wine press
>   much too long—
> Rebel! Rebel!
> We've got to rebel, y'all . . .

By now, with any luck, these words are true for you: you *refuse*, now and forevermore, to be what someone else wants you to be. If they aren't true, step boldly forward and *make* them true. Reclaim your God-given birthright: the freedom to do what you want to do with your life. This is your Crazy Dog activity for today, and tomorrow, and the rest of your natural life.

It's going to cause some chaos from time to time, of course—living truthfully always does. But keep on keepin' on, and out of the ashes and rubble you'll rise—a uniquely provocative, divinely inspired, ridiculously happy, old-fashioned, new-fangled, bona fide Crazy Dog.